Teenage Mothers: Their Experience, Strength, and Hope

by Andre Beauchamp
translated by Rosemarie Fisher, S.M.

RESOURCE PUBLICATIONS, INC.
San Jose, California

Editorial director: Kenneth Guentert
Managing editor: Kathi Drolet
Cover design: Terri Ysseldyke-All
Production Assistant: Elizabeth J. Asborno

First edition ©1988 Les Editions Bellarmin, Saint Laurent, Montreal, Canada
©1990 Resource Publications, Inc. All rights reserved. For reprint permission, write to:

Reprint Department
Resource Publication, Inc.
160 E. Virginia St., #290
San Jose, CA 95112-5848

Library of Congress Cataloging in Publication Data
Beauchamp, André 1938-
   [Mères célebataires. English]
   Teenage mothers : their experience, strength, and hope / by Andre Beauchamp; translated by Rosemarie Fisher.
      p. cm.
   Translation of: Mères célebataires.
   ISBN 0-89390-180-6: $8.95
   1. Teenage mothers—Canada. 2. Teenage mothers—United States.
3. Motherhood—Religious aspects—Christianity. 4. Misericordia Sisters.
   I. Title.
HQ759.4.B4213   1990
   306.85'6—dc20   90-38476
                                                            CIP

1 2 3 4 5 | 94 93 92 91 90

Scripture quotations are taken from *The Jerusalem Bible,* ©1966 Doubleday & Company, Inc., Garden City, New York.

The Magnificat is taken from *Psalms Anew,* by Maureen Leach, O.S.F., and Nancy Schreak, O.S.F., ©1984 Sisters of St. Francis, Dubuque, Iowa.

*...iation about the Misericordia
...se contact:*

Sr. Rosemarie Fisher, sm
c/o Rosalie Manor, Inc.
4803 West Burleigh Street
Milwaukee, WI 53210
(414) 449-2868

Contents

Foreword

Our culture these days is bombarded with statistics. It is so easy to give percentages of the population that are hurting in one way or another. So often then we are asked to make decisions on the basis of such statistics, decisions that affect the lives and the future of so many.

One step, however, is missing in this process: The statistics have to take on human faces before any healing can take place. Behind each number are often many faces, each one differing from the other, each one hurting in a different way than a neighbor. Each person is unique: each hurt is unique.

For statistics to take on human faces we have to listen to each one who is hurting and to the unique story that each one brings. We also must recognize that those closest to those hurting are the best for interpreting to us the needs they experience and the wounds they touch. No global formula works when applied, without discrimination, to all.

We can learn from a book such as this who those faces are behind the statistics; we can listen to their pain and sorrow; we can vicariously touch them and the reality of their wounds through their testimony. They must be listened to and those who touch them must also tell their story.

To both the wounded and the healer, it is the role of society to bring hope, strength, and courage. A book such as this is the way to begin our listening and to understand who owns those faces lying behind the statistics and how we can begin to help them and to bring them hope.

+ Rembert G.Weakland, O.S.B.
Archbishop of Milwaukee

Preface

Today, as Yesterday, Discovering Life Together

A Word from the Misericordia Sisters

Our history can be told as a fairy tale—not only a fairy tale about adversity, shame, and despair but also a fairy tale about hope, joy, and life.

Where it all began

Once upon a time there was a woman, Marie Rosalie Cadron. She was born at Lavaltrie, Quebec, Canada, on January 27, 1794. She was married on October 7, 1811, to John Marie Jette. She gave birth to eleven children, of whom five died at a young age. The six who survived were four boys and two girls. In 1832, her husband died of cholera.

Marie Rosalie Cadron's mother had been a midwife, and Marie Rosalie became one, too, in addition to carrying the heavy burden of maintaining her family. Marie Rosalie faced her widowhood with a renewed sense of dedication and devoted herself to works of charity. In May 1845, the bishop of the diocese of Montreal, Ignatius Bourget, asked her to focus her work on the needs of unwed mothers. This request led to the founding of the congregation of the Misericordia Sisters.

In the land of shame

In 1845, a single pregnant woman was judged harshly and treated with scorn. Her child was rejected as if cursed. Both the unwed mother and her illegitimate child were symbols of error and sin. Society rejected them as if they were carriers of a contagious disease. Whether it happened in the upper classes, in good Christian towns, or in the city slums, the attitude was the same: unwed mothers were evil, their children damned.

Whatever we may think, things haven't changed much. The old curse is still with us today, imposing a heavy burden on its victims. In Montreal or New York, Milwaukee or Toronto, Gatineau or Winnipeg, conventional society can still think of economic, social, and moral reasons to maintain the taboos and continue the same rejection.

In the land of hope

At first glance, you might assume that the world of the single mother is a living hell. Without doubt, it is a world of hidden suffering, but it is also a world of quiet miracles! Since the days of Rosalie Jette, we Misericordia Sisters have been constantly amazed by the joy, hope, and tenacity of these women who carry life within them and who triumph in life. Their journey on the slow and difficult road to maturity and understanding is a marvel of tenderness, compassion, and non-violence. It is an affirmation of life.

About the Misericordia Sisters

This small book is not an account of what the daughters of Rosalie Cadron Jette do for single mothers. Certainly we are motivated by a religious conviction and are convinced of God's love for us. God is love. In Jesus, the beloved Son, God gives us unlimited tenderness. We are offered salvation, joy, and peace. This conviction gives us life and compels us to respond to God's love by giving love. If we work with unmarried parents and their children, it is because in their great suffering we hear the incessant call, "I have seen the suffering of my people."

About single mothers

This book is primarily a picture of what single mothers experience today: their struggles, their hopes, their discoveries, their joys, their sorrows. They show us how they take hold of their lives as women and mothers in today's society, and how, through their experience, they discover the depth of life, life rooted in God.

Their lives give us life, pose questions for us, upset our standards, transform our hearts, and rejuvenate us. We believe that the complex paths that crisscross between them and us and from them and us to Jesus Christ also involve you, the reader. Life's paths are always open-ended.

A fairy tale?

This book is neither a fairy tale nor a horror story but rather a reflection of our hope built on dreams and flesh and blood, as is all of life.

The challenge we share is to discover life together.

Real-life stories

Many of the events and life situations described in this book are authentic. For reasons of confidentiality, names, places, times, and some circumstances have been changed. Some narratives reflect the stories of several people. They are based on experiences lived in the various places in Canada and the United States where the Misericordia Sisters minister.

The Sisters offer multiple services: pregnancy prevention programs, residential care before and after delivery, outpatient clinics, educational day care for children, social services, counseling, and home visiting.

The great variety of circumstances, needs, and services don't allow us to generalize. The Misericordia Sisters are dedicated to all women and their experience of motherhood, but especially to the single mother. Usually, she is young, has never been married, and has been deserted by her partner, who left when he was faced with the responsibility of a child. The increasing divorce rate means we also meet many women who find themselves alone and, as single parents, must raise their children alone. Each woman's needs are a little different, even if each one faces some of the same difficulties. Nevertheless, whatever the context or circumstances, there is suffering, and in all adversity, there is a call.

Living mercy

The Misericordia Sister is called to live the mercy of Jesus, the Savior, with young girls and women who are pregnant out of wedlock, with their children, and with married women who find it difficult to live their pregnancy. The Misericordia Sister acknowledges her total dependence on God's merciful love. Therefore, her whole life tends to become praise, adoration, and supplication of this merciful love (*Constitution and Observances of the Misericordia Sisters, nos. 3 and 4*).

A Word from the Author

Hats off to you!

I am a priest. In working on this book, I had access to different writings of the Misericordia Sisters and personal accounts of many single mothers. I was astounded by the depth and intensity of the personal comments I found. Three things in particular struck me.

The first was the importance of motherhood in a woman's life. Men know little about those things. They can barely guess at them. It is from the depths of her body, in the greatest intimacy of her being, that a woman forms a child and enters into a moving dialogue. Men's contempt and society's scorn of the single pregnant woman are usually just a way for people to flee from their responsibilities. Often the single mother has a negative image of herself, a pervasive sense of guilt. But, fortunately, she also demonstrates a courage and generosity that are beyond belief. Hats off to you!

The second thing that struck me was the gratitude and affection they have for the Misericordia Sisters. The initial feeling is that of being welcomed without being judged and of being loved and accepted as they are. Next, they are pleased with the varied services they receive: material help, a roof over their head, meals, professional help such as social services, psychological counseling, classes, medical assistance, referrals to other agencies, and day care. They are pleased to become part of a family with other young women, who come from different places and with whom they are able to talk, share, and celebrate holidays such as Christmas and Halloween. And, finally, most are thankful for the religious experience. Whatever their religion, they discover God anew and the power of God's forgiveness, presence, and love. It is like breaking out of one's prison and being able to say "Yes" to life. Again, hats off to you!

The third thing that struck me is the fact that the work of the Misericordia Sisters meets the needs of our time so well. Fortunately, over the last thirty years, our society has grown more aware of the needs of different groups of people. Policies to create a better society have been implemented in many places and in a variety of ways. But improvement takes more than that. It takes love. It takes stability. And even more, it takes hope. We need services that are rooted in the depth of human experience, grounded in the source of all love. In this regard, faith in Jesus Christ never ceases to surprise us by giving birth to foolish undertakings. The Misericordia Sisters are this kind of folly. Though recruitment seems at a crisis point, hopefully other solutions will emerge. I am confident in that hope, and with faith in the Lord, I say, my hat is off to you!

THE FORGIVEN AND LOVING WOMAN
(Luke 7:36-50)

One of the Pharisees invited him to a meal. When he arrived at the Pharisee's house and took his place at table, a woman came in who had a bad name in town. She had heard he was dining with the Pharisee and had brought with her an alabaster jar of ointment. She waited behind him at his feet, weeping, and her tears fell on his feet, and she wiped them away with her hair; then she covered his feet with kisses and anointed them with the ointment.

When the Pharisee who had invited him saw this, he said to himself, "If this man were a prophet, he would know who this woman is that is touching him and what a bad name she has." Then Jesus took him up and said, "Simon, I have something to say to you." "Speak, Master," was the reply. "There was once a creditor who had two men in his debt; one owed him five hundred denarii, the other fifty. They were unable to pay, so he pardoned them both. Which of them will love him more?" "The one who was pardoned more, I suppose," answered Simon. Jesus said, "You are right."

Then he turned to the woman. "Simon," he said, "you see this woman? I came into your house, and you poured no water over my feet, but she has poured out her tears over my feet and wiped them away with her hair. You gave me no kiss, but she has been covering my feet with kisses ever since I came in. You did not anoint my head with oil, but she has anointed by feet with ointment. For this reason I tell you that her sins, her many sins, must have been forgiven her, or she would not have shown such great love. It is the man who is forgiven little who shows little love." Then he said to her, "Your sins are forgiven." Those who were with him at table began to say to themselves, "Who is this man, that he even forgives sins?" But he said to the woman, "Your faith has saved you; go in peace."

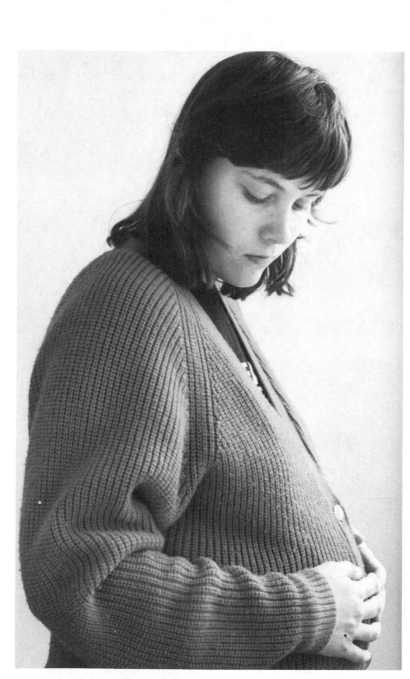

Ben Mark Holzberg

1

Rejection

Trying to Tell

"Mom, do you have five minutes? I have to talk to you."

"Not now, I'm watching my favorite program. You can talk to me later tonight."

"For once, we're all alone, Mom. I have to talk to you now."

"What's the matter?"

"Well, my period is late."

"That happens to every girl. Do you have cramps?"

"No, that's just it. I don't have any cramps."

"How many days are you late?"

"It's three months now."

"What? Are you crazy? Are you telling me you're pregnant? And it's already three months?"

"Mom, I didn't think I was pregnant. I just thought I was late."

"But, if you're pregnant, that means you've had sex."

"That's right, Mom. But I didn't think I could get pregnant."

"And who is the father?"

"It's Danny."

"How old is Danny?"

"Nineteen."

"What's he going to do?"

"He said he didn't want anything to do with a baby and that if I have the baby, it's my problem, not his."

"And what are you going to do?"

"I don't know."

"Maybe we could help you get an abortion."

"But, Mom, you always said you were against abortion."

"Of course I am against abortion, in general. But if my sixteen-year-old daughter who isn't married is pregnant and the child's father has run scared, it's different. I don't need an unwed mother in my family. That's the limit."

We could rewrite this scene in many ways: Gail, beaten within an inch of her life by her mother, or Latonya, raped five months earlier by her stepfather and now abandoned. Barbara is thrown out of the house. Maggie goes to live with her grandparents. Claire talks to one of her high school teachers, who helps her find an understanding social worker. Catherine goes to an abortion clinic, but it is closed that morning and the police are arresting some protesters. Kimberly receives loving support from her mother and the whole family. Julie, whose mother was a prostitute, follows in her mother's footsteps.

Every young woman who is single and pregnant needs support, guidance, and a sensitive listener. Something wondrous is happening inside her, yet she is usually rejected by those around her.

My most difficult memory

"When I was pregnant, I didn't have anyone to count on."

"My pregnancy destroyed the image I had of myself; it destroyed all my plans for the future."

"I saw Vince run away and knew that he never really cared for me."

"My pregnancy! It cut me off from my family and friends."

Being Rejected

The most difficult experience for the single mother is rejection.

Lisa doesn't use the word "boyfriend." Instead, like many single mothers, she talks about the father of her baby.

"My pregnancy was a very difficult time because the father of my baby refused to accept the fact that I was pregnant. He rejected the child and continually blamed me for the pregnancy."

In most cases, the single mother hasn't known the beauty and power of a mutual relationship. The child was conceived by accident, and now she must assume all the responsibility.

"When I was four months pregnant, I had to stop working. I found that very hard because I had always worked with people. From one day to the next, I didn't have anyone to talk to. I was without money, without support. The shape of my body was changing, and I thought of myself as fat and ugly."

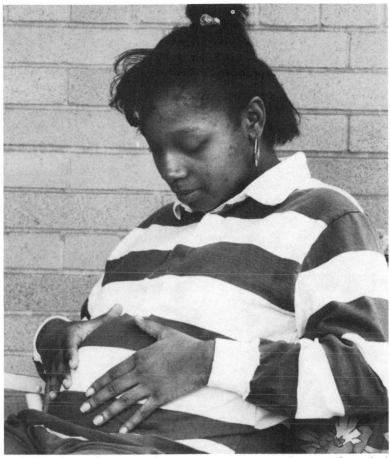

Georgeen Comerford

In other cases, this feeling of deep loneliness sets in after the relationship fails.

> "Jack just told me he was leaving. He didn't give any explanation. It was the weekend after Dawn's baptism. She was only two-and-a-half months old. I had always expected we would raise the child as a couple, not that I would be doing it all alone."

"I never dreamed that one day I would be a single parent. When Peter left me, I had to accept it and put up with the pain in order to get on with living."

"The father of my child was alcoholic, violent, spiteful. It was hard to leave him, but I had to do it."

"My boyfriend left in the middle of the night, when I was eight months pregnant. I thought I was going to die. After a year of living together, he took all his things and walked out on me in the middle of the night. The situation was overwhelming. In one week, I lost twelve pounds. He came back just when I was going to deliver, but said that he would leave again as soon as the baby was born. He was there at the delivery and kept his word. He left!"

Georgeen Comerford

"I had an abortion. I had been going with my boyfriend for two years, and he simply refused to talk about my pregnancy, saying that it was my problem. At the time, I didn't feel I was able to raise a child alone. The abortion was painful, physically and psychologically.

"The same thing happened to me several years later. I met someone and became pregnant almost at the start of our relationship. He was married and hadn't told me. I had a lot of illusions. The first two months of my pregnancy were difficult. I was studying and working at the same time. I had to make a decision and I had to make it all alone. I didn't want to live through another abortion. Life was stronger than death this time. Once I made the decision to have the baby, I was relieved, and after that, things went smoothly."

THE ADULTEROUS WOMAN
(John 8:1-11)

Jesus went to the Mount of Olives.

At daybreak he appeared in the Temple again; and as all the people came to him, he sat down and began to teach them.

The scribes and Pharisees brought a woman along who had been caught committing adultery; and making her stand there in full view of everybody, they said to Jesus, "Master, this woman was caught in the very act of committing adultery, and Moses has ordered us in the Law to condemn women like this to death by stoning. What have you to say?" They asked him this as a test, looking for something to use against him. But Jesus bent down and started writing on the ground with his finger. As they persisted with their question, he looked up and said, "If there is one of you who has not sinned, let him be the first to throw a stone at her." Then he bent down and wrote on the ground again. When they heard this, they went away one by one, beginning with the eldest, until Jesus was left alone with the woman, who remained standing there. He looked up and said, "Woman, where are they? Has no one condemned you?" "No one, sir," she replied. "Neither do I condemn you," said Jesus. "Go away, and don't sin anymore."

ONE FAMILIAR WITH SUFFERING
(Isaiah 53:2-4)

Like a sapling he grew up in front of us,
    like a root in arid ground.
Without beauty, without majesty
    no looks to attract our eyes;
a thing despised and rejected by everyone,
a man of sorrows and familiar with suffering,
a man to make people screen their faces,
    he was despised and we took no account of him.
And yet ours were the sufferings he bore,
    ours the sorrows he carried.
But we, we thought of him as someone punished,
    struck by God and brought low.

Ben Mark Holzberg

2

Being a Mother

A Mother's Joy

Without always understanding what is happening, the single pregnant woman has made some choices.

In the first place, she didn't use any type of birth control because she didn't know enough about them, she chose not to use them, or she was unable to use them. Many young women don't understand the rhythm of their bodies, and many know even less about the methods and the discipline necessary to control conception.

Once pregnant, the single mother chose not to have an abortion. That choice may have been made for religious reasons or simply because abortion facilities were not available. Sometimes, the single mother chooses not to have an abortion because she feels that she is ready for motherhood. Most often, however, it's because instinctively, intuitively, the desire for life is stronger than anything else.

My most beautiful memory

"My most beautiful memory? It was in the recovery room, after my Cesarean section. I opened my eyes and saw my son beside me. It's almost unbelievable that this fragile little being could come from me. And that I carried him inside my body for nine months."

"The delivery is a unique experience. I suffered a lot when I gave birth to Nathan, but to see this little being eased all the pain."

"My son was born with his left foot malformed. My most beautiful memory?

It's to see him walking normally today. He had surgery, orthopedic shoes, prostheses—and now, his foot is straight. It's fantastic."

"I gave life to someone. It means suffering, but what a reward! It's unforgettable."

(*This testimony is from a father.*) "Being present at the birth of my son made me feel a joy I had never known before. It was as if I were dreaming. It felt as if I had always known this little person, that I had always been waiting for him. At long last, I witnessed a miracle."

"My most beautiful memory? Having two beautiful children, knowing two beautiful pregnancies!"

"When I was carrying Cory during the seven months of my pregnancy. You see, I can't have another child."

"I have experienced some beautiful things in my life, but nothing ever really touched me until I saw Patrick for the first time in the hospital. I was happy, but at the same time a little sad, to bring him into the world in the circumstances I was in."

"After a long labor, seeing the fruits of my efforts. I held my baby, still attached to me by the umbilical cord, before he was even bathed. I cried. I didn't feel the pain anymore, only joy."

"To hold my baby in my arms for the first time.
To feed, caress, and talk to her.

To have felt her living inside of, and now,
   to see her face to face.
To know she has been made in my body.
To establish a unique mother-child
   relationship.
Even if I'm alone,
Even if I'm not married,
Even if I am rejected by society,
This whole experience, those first minutes,
   those first hours,
      those first days,
are something absolutely extraordinary."

Portrait

She just turned fourteen. Her father is Black and her mother, Hispanic. They bring together in a common destiny all the forms of poverty found in the inner city.

She just turned fourteen. She has the dreams of a child. She wants more freedom, music that never ends, mornings to sleep in, all night dancing, peace in the world and between people, an easy life. The most beautiful day of her life was her brother's graduation. It was wonderful! The whole family was there. There were uncles, aunts, and friends, the sun, a lavish meal, plenty for everyone—and everyone was relaxed, friendly, and attentive to one another.

She is still a child. She's lonesome for her parents in spite of their poverty. She's happy to have people care about what's happening to her, to talk to other girls, to see a nurse, to see a social worker, and to continue her schooling so she can graduate from eighth grade.

She just turned fourteen. She is only a child, but with the body of a woman, not yet fully developed but developed enough so that her womanhood can be proven. She came to the Misericordia Sisters at the suggestion of a social worker. At the home, she really doesn't like the rules or the responsibility of cleaning her room, which she shares with another girl and which is more comfortable than anything she ever knew in her family's inner-city tenement.

She is only fourteen. Nevertheless, in this little girl's abdomen, something is moving and growing, pushing against the fleshy wall of her womb, stretching, letting its will be known. And this woman-child feels within her this other child, who is making her become a mother. She's scared, overwhelmed, but she understands that something wonderful and awesome is happening.

If this young woman knocked at your door, what would you do? The Misericordia Sisters simply opened their door and are journeying with this child who is becoming a mother.

Barb Lynch

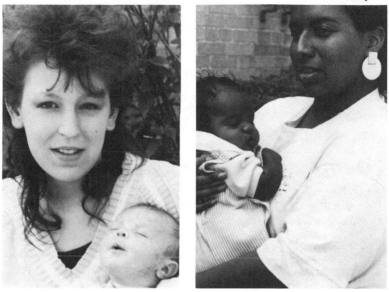

What Do We Have in Common?

Tell me, Mary,
What do we have in common,
   You and me?
People look at me with suspicion,
   With lots of hidden meanings.
Me, the single, unwed mother,
   A bit of a gypsy, a little lost,
   Now a good mother, now bad.
I carry my child in the storm,
   Without knowing if I love or hate him,
   If I am loving him well
   Or loving him badly,
   If my child will succeed in life.

Being a Mother

Tell me, Mary,
    Did you ever on an evening
    Breathe the heavy odor of incense and perfumes,
    Pungent fumes that captivate?
Here, they call them drugs;
    They're really bad for you,
    But for an hour, only an hour,
    It's as if a corner of heaven
    Opened just for you.

Tell me, Mary,
    Did you ever feel
    People's looks when you were pregnant?
Those who look at you out of the corner of their eye,
    Or turn to look once you have passed by,
    And who say under their breath,
    Look she's not married!
At least you had Joseph.
Still, at Bethlehem
    You had to go from place to place,
    From door to door,
Because there was no place that would welcome you
    Except a hidden corner
    Among the animals.

Good Mary, Holy Mary, journey with me.
    You know how much I like men,
    Even mine
    Who is brutal, macho,
    And who thinks he must
    Be hard, scornful, egotistical
    In order to look like a man.

When I see a man,
  I hate to admit it,
  I feel warm all over.
  I tremble like a leaf in the wind.
  I'm all excited,
  Upset, surprised,
And the turmoil of my flesh overpowers the voice of
  the heart.
I want love so much.
I want understanding, respect, tenderness.
I want to be free, independent.
I want a love that is shared by equals,
  Yet I am always a slave to my own desire.

Mary,
Brave Mary,
Holy Mary,
You, whose body became the temple of the Spirit,
  We have so many things in common.
Give me light and strength;
Lead me to the paths of joy.

And Life Continues

"Eric is so stubborn. I find he can be
obstinate and slow to understand. It is as if
he is looking for ways to annoy me. But, at
the same time, he is very affectionate and
loving. I wouldn't change him for anything
in the world. He's the most beautiful gift
God ever gave me."

"I don't want him to be like me, at least
not totally. I want him to be happy and full
of life. I hope that his life will be better
than mine; that he will be happy with

19

himself; that he won't have to live on welfare as I do; that he will find a good job that he likes; that he will meet a woman who will love him the way he wants to be loved."

"I have three children. Three surprise packages. My first child has suffered a lot because he wasn't with his mother for the first year of his life. It seems to me he has had trouble learning to love because of this. But I can see a lot of progress in him now. My second child is a girl. People pressured me to reject her even before her birth, so much so that I was depressed during the pregnancy. It was my third child that made me come to my senses. He was also unexpected, but as soon as I knew he was there inside me, I welcomed him. It seems to me that from that moment, many things changed for me. I felt real peace, a new capacity to love."

"I felt tremendous pain the day life separated me from my partner. For him, it was the end of his despair; for me, the beginning of a nightmare of utter misery. I couldn't accept it. It's hard to accept life as a single parent."

"I learned to love my child, but there are still times I'd like to be alone again. I didn't want to have a daughter, but when I had her, I asked God to give me the strength and courage I needed. I didn't want her to experience what I had experienced: abandonment. At my daughter's age, I was already separated from my mother. I was eighteen when I had my daughter, who is now four years old and is still—with her mother."

"I became a mother at seventeen. Today I understand that I was still a child myself. To escape reality, I drank and took drugs because I was sick in my soul. I was searching and made a lot of mistakes. But, at some point, everyone has to face reality. I now have three children. The oldest, David, is ten and beginning the pre-teen stage. At first I just had him to look after. But now, with Steven (three years old) and Joanne (four months old), I'm overwhelmed. It's no fun. I'm afraid that David will feel less loved because his mother doesn't have time anymore."

"I have changed a lot. Before, I was not conscious of what I was or who I was. Thanks to this experience, I'm learning to take care of someone else, to be responsible. Above all, I want to grow, mature, and accept my life. I'm discovering my limitations and learning how to live with them. I'm also learning to forgive myself."

"As I watch my child grow, I understand life better—my parents' life and my own. I am more human and more patient."

"When I gave birth to my child, it was as if I came into the world myself. Teaching my child was also teaching myself. My child has taught me so much about my own strengths and my weaknesses. That has made me grow up a lot."

Barb Lynch

"I have the impression that I've changed.
Perhaps it's really not true. I can still get
carried away by flattery and false promises.
I made a resolution never to believe a guy's
words again."

"After twenty-seven years of working at
it, my mother and I have finally learned
how to communicate. I can even say that
we have become friends, just like I always
wanted."

LIKE A SON
COMFORTED BY HIS MOTHER
(Isaiah 66:12-13)

Now towards her I send flowing
    peace, like a river,
    and like a stream in flood
    the glory of the nations.
At her breast will her nurslings be carried
    and fondled in her lap.
    Like a son comforted by his mother
    Will I comfort you.

Barb Lynch

THE PATH TO JOY
(John 16:21-22)

"A woman in childbirth suffers, because her time has come; but when she has given birth to the child she forgets the suffering in her joy that a person has been born into the world. So it is with you: you are sad now, but I shall see you again, and your hearts will be full of joy, and that joy no one shall take from you."

MARY SINGS HER JOY
(The Magnificat)

My being proclaims your greatness, and my spirit
  finds joy in you, God my Savior.

For you have looked upon your servant in my
  lowliness; all ages to come shall call me blessed.

God, you who are mighty, have done great things
  for me;
  Holy is your name.

Your mercy is from age to age toward those who
  fear you.

You have shown might with your arm and confused
  the proud in their inmost thoughts.

You have deposed the mighty from their thrones
  and raised the lowly to high places.

The hungry you have given every good thing, while
  the rich you have sent empty away.

You have upheld Israel, your servant, ever mindful
  of your mercy

Even as you promised our ancestors, promised
  Abraham, Sarah, and their descendants forever.

3

Making a New Life

Danuta

When Danuta came to Montreal, she was almost at the end of her rope.

Danuta immigrated to Canada eight years ago. As a mother of two children, she was surviving pretty well. Then her partner left her, and the wandering began. She lived out of shopping bags, wore rags, and accepted handouts just to get by. On sunny days, when it was warm, the children played without worry, but on rainy days, they had to find shelter and put up with people's strange looks. On cold days, they chose to keep walking rather than sit down on park benches for fear of losing the last little bit of warmth they had.

She and her children lived the wandering life of vagabonds. The police arrested her because her children looked neglected and because the city needed cleaning up. But beyond arresting her, what could they do? Preach to her? Explain to her that living on the street is a one-way route to a life of alcohol, drugs, prostitution, and misery? Threaten her with prison? But then, who would take care of the children? What work could Danuta do? What experience did she have? What inner strengths did she have?

The judicial system cannot spend time and money dealing with these questions. She was sent to a social worker who referred Danuta and the two children to the Misericordia Sisters. Now she had a room, a good bed, adequate meals, hot water, a sense of security for at least three days, someone to help take care of the children, time to talk to other women who were trying to break out of poverty, and time to talk with social workers.

She began the hard road back by taking responsibility for herself, putting some order into her life, living more consciously, stopping her abuse of drugs and alcohol, applying for welfare. Within two weeks she needed to find a place to live. She had to take that step into the real world, no matter how humble a step. She had to refuse to panic, learn the language of the country and how to communicate properly. After six months to a year, maybe she could get a job and stop smoking. Maybe she could care for the children in a new way: take them to the day care center in the morning, bring them home in the evening, watch them grow and change. And once a week, she could return to the Center to talk and share life. She knew now that in times of hard knocks, depression, or emergencies, somewhere there would be a friend, a social worker, a Misericordia Sister ready to help.

There are Danutas who never overcome their situation. There are Danutas who do. It depends primarily on courage. But it's also a matter of meeting people at the right moment who can help you take a new hold on reality and give you a little trust, a little help, a little love, and a little self-confidence.

Adoption

"Several years ago, I gave birth to a handicapped child. I couldn't give him all the care he needed. With the help of the Misericordia Sisters, I quickly understood the real problem and the obligations I would be taking on. I decided to give my child for adoption in a specialized hospital where he could have all the proper care. It was a very hard decision to make, especially because those around me didn't understand why I did it."

"I gave my child for adoption. I really appreciated the psychological help I had in making this decision, which was the best one for me to make in my situation. But even after the adoption was final, I felt depressed on my child's birthday. After five years I still do! Now and then, I wish his adoptive parents would send a picture of him or some news about his health, his schooling, everything he's doing. It would have to be done anonymously, but I think it would help me. If he died, I wouldn't even know about it!"

"The day I gave my child for adoption was the hardest day of my life. I knew in my head it was best. But I still wonder, after all these years, what has become of my child."

Barb Lynch

Barb Lynch

Sometimes Love

The following is an excerpt from a letter to a Misericordia Sister.

"The last time we spoke, I was getting ready for the wedding. Now we've been married a year in November, and everything is going well between Andy and me. God has blessed our marriage. Andy is now the assistant manager at a restaurant in a shopping center, and I still work with the children at the day care center.

"But my big news is that I'm pregnant. Eleven years ago, expecting a child didn't bother me at all. Now, at twenty-six, I'm not sure I'm ready to accept this responsibility. Even worse, I feel self-conscious about being pregnant. I forgot what it felt like. I guess we only remember happy things. I keep telling Andy that I'm not going through another pregnancy and that we'll adopt our second one! I know that's not really true. I'm so happy that we are able to have children. But I keep remembering the past, and that clouds the present. When I knew I was pregnant this time, I felt guilty, as though I had done something wrong. It's strange that I should feel that way now, when I never felt like that the first time, eleven years ago.

"In spite of that, I'm very happy. And I have more plans than I know what to do with..."

Paul Hamel, SJ

"What I have found the most difficult is trying to raise my child alone. What's more, my family continually rejected me, and my daughter's father was really hard on me. Now I'm in love. We're going to be married this summer. He's an extraordinary man—gentle, simple, someone who already acts like a perfect father for my little girl. I never thought I'd ever want to get married. Life is full of surprises...even at thirty-five!"

What Is the Child's Name?

Carl.
Jeannine.
Cynthia.
Brenda.
Catherine.
Linda.
Ebony.
David.
Sandra.

Jonathon.
Donovan.
Tanya.
Christopher.
Patrick.
Donna.
Shannon.
Matthew.
Julie.

Each child is a unique mystery, a personal story. Between each child and mother is another story—complex, mysterious, full of emotion. The mystery of life. What is her name? What is his name? What will the future hold?

My Child

You are my night,
  The shadow of my past,
  The memory of a storm that was too strong,
  Of my wayward youth,
  Of my rebellion,
  Of my foolishness.

You are the flower of today,
  The laughter that fills the house,
  The sweet chaos of things,
  In days of joy,
  In days of tears,
  Even in days of sickness!
  As you grow,
  Our home stretches to include the whole world.

You are the sun of the future,
  The light that pulls us forward,
  The hope of better days,
  The reason to struggle, to work, to hang on
  Against the rain, against the storm,
  Even against exhaustion.

You are the window of life.
  My child,
  My dear daughter,
  My own likeness,
  We will journey together.

STRONGER THAN ANYTHING
(Romans 8:35-39)

Nothing therefore can come between us and the love of Christ, even if we are troubled or worried, or being persecuted, or lacking food or clothes, or being threatened or even attacked. As scripture promised: For your sake we are being massacred daily, and reckoned as sheep for the slaughter. These are the trials through which we triumph, by the power of him who loved us.

For I am certain of this: neither death nor life, no angel, no prince, nothing that exists, nothing still to come, not any power, or height or depth, nor any created thing, can ever come between us and the love of God made visible in Christ Jesus our Lord.

"WOMEN RISING"

Hear their voices rising as one,
    see their hands clasped together.
Watch their spirits resurrecting,
    seeking new horizons with courage and hope.

The rising is slow, but continuous,
    much like the rising of the sun, or bread.
Their heads are held high,
    symbolizing new pride, new inner strength!

They know what the real issue is—
    not drugs, not sex, not single parents—POVERTY.
Poverty is the real issue
    that strips them of their dignity!

Don't declare war on drugs—
    declare war on poverty—*again*—
    but this time don't tell them (the poor)
    they they must change—
    tell the *system* that it *must* change!!

"Women Rising" will bring
    hope through building
    up the individual;
    freeing the woman to discover her
    possibilities—her own inner strength.

With strength, women will
unite—single mothers will unite—
changes will happen "out there"
because changes have happened
in the hearts and souls of single mothers.

They will no longer see themselves
as "the scourge of the city"—

they, together, will find their
individual and collective beauty.

Women are arising—through their
   discovery of "we can" and the
   nurturance of each other, women are
   rising—and once resurrection
   takes place, there is no going back
   to the tomb!

   —Melissa Butts, O.P.
     Social Worker, Rosalie Manor, Milwaukee

4

Meeting God

Georgeen Comerford

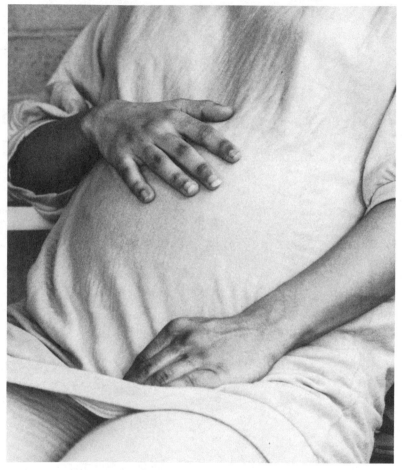

Paths to God

Many and varied are the paths to God!
But for the single pregnant woman
   Whose parents reject her,
   At whom society points a finger,
For the woman abandoned,
   The paths to God
   Are not often easy or straight.
They are full of detours,
   Change and confusion.
But yet, they lead to the water of life,
   Water that flows
   From the source of eternal life.

Everyone wants to succeed in life,
   To be happy above all else,
   To have everything go well,
   To have peace and harmony,
   Easy mutual understanding,
   And maybe—Why not?—
   To have God to bless it all.
Isn't God on the side of happy people
   Who are prosperous,
   Who live successful lives,
   Who lead holy, righteous, worthy lives?
The God of the strong, the holy, the honest,
The God of winners?

It takes very little for our world to crumble:
   A little misfortune, an illness, a loss,
   A moment of rebellion, an instant of weakness,
   A voice that whispers,
   "Take and taste this fruit!
You'll become like gods,
   Knowing good and evil" (Genesis 3:5).
We worship money!

We talk about it so much in our world.
We need it so much for so many things.
We're so miserable when we don't have enough.
A little money for a small piece of my soul—
     Is that so bad?
We surrender to the dream of glory!
To be the first, to be the best,
To be the boss for once,
To be a star, the center of attention,
     The object of desire,
To make our will the rule for others,
To be for one hour, just one hour, a Michael, a
     Madonna, an Elvis,
To see oneself, just once, on television.
And the voice said,
     "This world will be yours if you adore me"
     (Luke 4:7).

At one time or another
     For everyone, for every believer,
     There is a descent into hell,
     A failure, brokenness, weakness,
     At twenty or at fifty!
And then the long journey that leads to God begins.
Single mothers precede us on this path.
First comes the experience of rejection,
     Suffering,
     The belief that everyone is against you,
     The cold contemptuous looks,
     Other looks, loaded with anger,
     And the terrible, boundless solitude.
Suffering, frightened, diminished
     In heart and in body,
     Without family,
     Not knowing who you are any more.
And then, like a candle's flame in the midst of the
     night,

You encounter a smile,
    Share a cup of coffee, a cigarette,
    Dare to have a conversation,
To feel a presence,
To experience God in sharing
    In kindness, in mercy,
    In forgiveness,
To understand, as if they were your own,
    The tender stories of
    The Samaritan woman, the prodigal son,
    The lost coin.
"Go and learn the meaning of the words:
    What I want is mercy, not sacrifice"
    (Matthew 9:13).

Then the long road to forgiveness begins.
First forgiveness of oneself:
    Relearning to love,
    Finding a more positive self-image,
    Discovering a lost sense of personal dignity,
    Knowing that you are reconciled with God,
    Humbly welcoming God's forgiveness,
    And, at last, slowly, with difficulty,
    Beginning to forgive others:
Father, mother,
The man who didn't know,
    Didn't understand, couldn't,
    Wouldn't.
Throughout life,
    A compelling light draws one to the words,
    "Father, forgive them, they do not know what
    they are doing" (Luke 23:34).

And then the others:
    This child, first of all, so fragile,
    This little girl, this small boy,
    This selfish being who snatches life in your womb,

Frank Miller

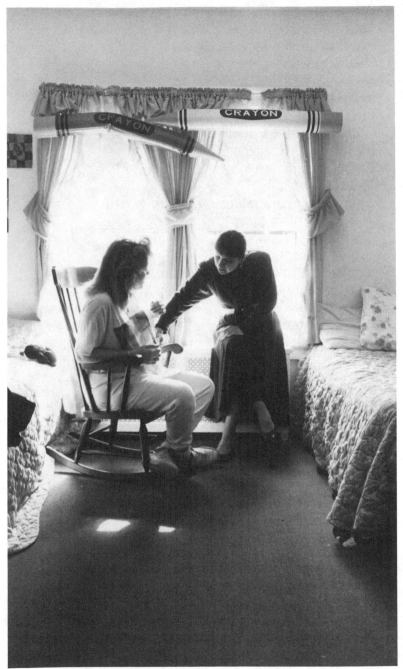

Who is born of your flesh,
Who owns your body, your nights, your life,
And whose smallest smile can overpower you;
    This child who makes you better than you are,
Who pulls you forward
Beyond yourself
In the immense adventure of life.
Meeting other women
    Like yourself,
Searching for the light,
Joining your small flame to the flame of others,
    And from all these sparks, a bright fire grows.
Discovering things in common,
Discussing, talking, thinking, listening,
Laughing, singing,
Celebrating, dancing, crying, sharing,
Taking care of another mother's child for a whole
    evening,
Phoning someone when you know they're down,
Building community,
And, in the process, becoming Church.
    "By this love you have for one another,
    Everyone will know that you are my disciples"
    (John 13:35).

Then comes serenity.
The storm ceases to rage.
Like Christ awakening in the boat
    And calming the sea,
The woman awakens in the woman
    And calms her inner storm,
    Bringing peace and serenity to the world.
Why so much violence,
    So many senseless actions,
    So many wars, so many deaths?

Why this mania to uproot everything,
    To have, to possess,
    To separate the good from the bad,
    The weeds from the wheat,
    When everything is so deeply linked together?
To trust life,
To trust God.
It's still not harvest time,
    But rather a time for patience,
    Another season's time
    Under God's sun,
    A time for prayer.
"Be brave, I have conquered the world"
    (John 16:33).

Many and varied are the ways to God.
Everyone follows her own path.
All along the journey,
    Our roads create themselves and then dissolve.
Often we seem lost;
    Sometimes we wander for a long time,
    Not knowing the road's destination.
Happy are the crossroads
    That help us to find signposts
    In God's country.
On my road, I found
    A homosexual,
    Two single mothers,
    Three divorced men,
    Four children,
    Five prisoners,
    Six who were ill,
    Seven alcoholics,
    Eight strangers,
    Nine who were poor,
    Ten who were unhappy!

The God they showed me
   Didn't look like the God I was seeking.
But the God who found me
   Looked very much like
   The poor who revealed God to me.
"I thank you, Father,
For hiding these things from the learned and wise
And revealing them to the simple" (Matthew 11:25).

To Forgive

"My father really destroyed me. He always told me I was foolish and stupid. He wouldn't let me go out or have any fun. Because of that, I never had any sense of independence. Now I think I'm able to forgive him. Life has taught me that we can only give what we are capable of giving. It's hard to love if we weren't loved well ourselves. But in forgiving, we learn slowly to love."

"When you haven't felt you were OK for years, you don't change overnight."

"Men have hurt me. A lot. I believed their words, but I was always disappointed. Now I accept all that's happened. Jesus' example gives me hope; he forgave his enemies."

"Six years ago, a man broke into my house and raped me. It's the worst thing that could happen to anyone. For a long time, I believed it would have been better if I'd killed myself. The fear will never leave me. Often people hurt others without even realizing it. I know we have to forgive them

Georgeen Comerford

and tell ourselves that we, too, could hurt
someone unintentionally, but I can't find
the strength to forgive that man."

"I forgive, but I have trouble forgetting.
With time, everything gets better if we
want it to. But there's always a bit of a scar
on the heart or on one's self-respect. I'm
still on the defensive."

God as a Friend

"Yes, I believe in God. In everyday life, in
the good times and in bad moments, I think
of God. I'm not really 'practicing,' but I
think that if you love, appreciate, and
respect others, yourself, and your
environment, God will not be far from you."

"God has a special place in my life. I
often think of God. When I look at Nick, I
say to myself, 'This must have happened
for a good reason.' But I don't go to
church."

"Yes, I believe in God. I have to admit,
I'm a little self-centered because I don't
talk to him often. But on the other hand, I
never forget to thank God if something
wonderful happens. In difficult times, I ask
for courage and strength to get through the
struggle."

"Yes, I believe in God, and God's place in
my life is greater than I would have
thought. I know how important that is, and
my life gets better as I come to know God.
I'm discovering that God is love. Before

this spiritual journey, I believed in God, but I was rebelling. Today, I'm reconciled with the Church, and I'm beginning to find its place in my life. It's two years now that I've been coming to the Christian journey reflection group."

"I believe there has to be a supreme being to create so many wonders. For example, just think, a male and a female cell join and a child is formed. That's beyond me! I thank God when good things happen in my life. I thank God for having stood by me. When misfortune happens, I ask for the strength to get through it."

"Yes, I believe in God. Having God in my life for me means putting love into all I do in everyday life. Having God in my life assures me that I will have moments of happiness. Sadly, though, that doesn't always happen. Often I stray from God and become proud, resentful, full of self-pity. But the more I grow, the more aware I become of my errors, and it gets easier to come back to the right road."

"I believe there is a God of love. God fills my thoughts and my whole life. God helps me when I ask for it. I speak and God listens; often God helps me to see things more clearly. After sharing with the group, I'm more open to God. It really helps me to understand my own spiritual journey."

"Yes, I believe in God. I'd like to think that God would always have the first place in my heart, in my life. But it isn't always like that. Sometimes God is in second, even third place. But I never forget God completely."

"I believe that all we have comes from and must return to God. The Psalms tell us that. We have to work hard, but everything is from God."

"Yes, I believe in God; you can't touch God, but God has always helped me to get through painful situations. God rekindles my courage, warms my heart. I try hard to stay in contact with God, but because God is so interior, it is hard to explain God's presence."

"For me, God is a friend. I share my joys and sorrows with God. I'm grateful every day for good health for both myself and my children. Sometimes I get angry at God because of my problems, but it's still easy to pray because I know God will understand."

"I believe in God. Very much! God holds a very important place in my everyday life. God is the only person that understands me without putting me down."

The Last Resort of the Poor

I'll say it bluntly:
  We, the poor, have nothing left.

If it needs to be written,
  We don't have the words,
  Or the grammar,
  Or beautiful phrases.
We scribble a few letters
  And that's all!

If it takes money,
  We don't have any!
It's well known
  That it takes money to make money.
We, we survive day to day,
  Waiting for the first of the month,
  Celebrating a bit too much
  When the check finally arrives.
The poor don't have any past or any future.

If a new company comes to the neighborhood,
  No one asks us about it.
They see the mayor, the city council,
  All the influential people.
We find out about it just a little too late.
And if we raise our voices,
  We quickly hear
  That we are only a fringe group
  Against progress,
  Or that political interests are
  Using us.

We are the champions
  Of the last place
  In file after file,
  In regulation after regulation,
  In news broadcast after news broadcast,
Except perhaps for two weeks
  Before a political election.

Thank God, though, for us, the poor.
As a last resort
  We still have prayer
When the boss says no
When the cop says no
When the landlord says no
When the politician says no
When the union says no
When the newspaper reporter says no
When the bank manager says no
Even when your own group says no
When nothing much is left—
  Nothing or almost nothing
  Nothing at all
  Less than nothing.

For us, the poor,
  What's left?
The street
The sidewalk
Crime
Fear.
And at the bottom, at the very bottom of it all,
  Dare we say it clearly,
  The ultimate last resort
  The secret message:
  Prayer!

From the bottom of the abyss
From the top of my hell
From the bottom of my misery
    When no one knows I even exist,
    I pray.
Hear my voice,
Speak to me,
    Because, from the depth of my misery,
    I cry, I shout, I plead.

There is nothing anymore:
    Silence, death, fear,
And yet, deep inside, a fragile light
    That I still dare to call prayer.
I say it with my whole being,
    From the pit of my stomach to my throat
    A cry rises up like unquenchable joy:
You are the God of the poor
    Forever more.

TALKING WITH THE
SAMARITAN WOMAN
(John 4:5-42)

On the way, he came to the Samaritan town called
Sychar, near the land that Jacob gave to his son
Joseph. Jacob's well is there, and Jesus, tired by his
journey, sat straight down by the well. It was about
the sixth hour. When a Samaritan woman came to
draw water, Jesus said to her, "Give me a drink."
His disciples had gone into the town to buy food.
The Samaritan woman said to him, "What? You are
a Jew and you ask me, a Samaritan, for a drink?"
Jews, in fact, do not associate with Samaritans.
Jesus replied, "If you only knew what God is offering
and who it is that is saying to you, 'Give me a drink,'
you would have been the one to ask, and he would
have given you living water."

"You have no bucket, sir," she answered, "and the
well is deep. How could you get this living water?
Are you a greater man than our father Jacob who
gave us this well and drank from it himself with his
sons and his cattle?"

Jesus replied: "Whoever drinks this water will get
thirsty again; but anyone who drinks the water that
I shall give will never be thirsty again: the water
that I shall give will turn into a spring inside him,
welling up to eternal life."

"Sir," said the woman, "give me some of that
water, so that I may never get thirsty and never
have to come here again to draw water."

"Go and call your husband," said Jesus to her,
"and come back here."

The woman answered, "I have no husband."

He said to her, "You are right to say, 'I have no
husband,' for although you have had five, the one

you have now is not your husband. You spoke the truth there."

"I see you are a prophet, sir," said the woman. "Our fathers worshiped on this mountain, while you say that Jerusalem is the place where one ought to worship."

Jesus said, "Believe me, woman, the hour is coming when you will worship the Father neither on this mountain nor in Jerusalem. You worship what you do not know; we worship what we do know; for salvation comes from the Jews. But the hour will come—in fact, it is here already—when true worshipers will worship the Father in spirit and truth: that is the kind of worshiper the Father wants. God is spirit, and those who worship must worship in spirit and truth."

The woman said to him, "I know that Messiah— that is, Christ—is coming; and when he comes he will tell us everything."

"I who am speaking to you," said Jesus, "I am he."

At this point his disciples returned and were surprised to find him speaking to a woman, though none of them asked, "What do you want from her?" or "Why are you talking to her?" The woman put down her water jar and hurried back to the town to tell the people, "Come and see a man who has told me everything I ever did; I wonder if he is the Christ?" This brought people out of the town and they started walking toward him.

Meanwhile, the disciples were urging him, "Rabbi, do have something to eat," but he said, "I have food to eat that you do not know about." So the disciples asked one another, "Has someone been bringing him food?"

But Jesus said, "My food is to do the will of the one who sent me, and to complete his work. Have you not got a saying: 'Four months and then the harvest'? Well, I tell you: Look around you, look at the fields; already they are white, ready for harvest! Already the reaper is being paid his wages, already he is bringing in the grain for eternal life, and thus sower and reaper rejoice together. For here the proverb holds good: 'One sows, another reaps'; I sent you to reap a harvest you had not worked for. Others worked for it; and you have come into the rewards of their trouble."

Many Samaritans of that town had believed in him on the strength of the woman's testimony when she said, "He told me all I have ever done," so, when the Samaritans came up to him, they begged him to stay with them. He stayed for two days, and when he spoke to them many more came to believe; and they said to the woman, "Now we no longer believe because of what you told us; we have heard him ourselves and we know that he really is the savior of the world."

5

The Child

What Will You Do in the Future?

It's eleven o'clock at night. Celine turns off the television and starts to get ready for bed. She sees a faint glimmer of light coming from the door of Peter's room. She approaches the room, quietly turns the doorknob, and opens the door.

Surprised, Peter quickly slips something under the covers.

"Peter, what were you doing?"

"Nothing, Mom."

"Then why is your light on?"

"I'm afraid of the dark."

"Peter, you know that's a lie. You're not afraid of the dark and you can't sleep with the light on. What are you doing?"

"Well, I was reading."

"What were you reading?"

"Stories."

"What stories?"

Celine is suspicious. Can a little, nine-year-old boy already be attracted to off-color magazines? Oh no, not at his age; it's too soon.

"Show me what you were reading."

"It's nothing, Mom."

"Peter, show me."

Peter's look is stubborn, but Celine doesn't back down. She wonders: are we going to have a scene? Screams, arguments, blows? Celine is worried, but she doesn't want to panic.

"Peter, trust me. I won't be angry. Show me what you're hiding."

Blushing, Peter does as he's told. He pulls out a race car magazine. Celine, who was fearing the prelude of adolescence, doesn't understand.

"Why did you want to hide that from me?"

"Because you're always afraid."

"Me, afraid?"

"Sure. When I cross the street, you tell me to watch out. When I take my bike out, you tell me you're worried. If I run, you're afraid I'll fall. You don't like it when I fight. You don't like me to play hockey."

"I'm afraid because I don't want you to hurt yourself. But why would you think I wouldn't want you to read stories about race car drivers?"

"You don't want me to be like my father. He was a truck driver."

"I didn't say that. What I meant was, I don't want you to act like your father, because he left us."

"Sure, but he was a truck driver."

"It's not because he was a truck driver, but because he wasn't a responsible person. Do you want to be a race car driver?"

"I don't know. But it sounds exciting."

"What do you want to be when you grow up?"

"I don't know. What do you want me to be, Mom?"

Celine thinks for a moment. Dare she say that she wants all the best for him? That he has a good education, that he succeeds in life, that he is the best? That he doesn't turn out like his father, or her father, or his uncles? That he doesn't become a drunkard, or vulgar? That he becomes a hard worker, disciplined, understanding? That he takes care of his mother and never abandons her? That he is always obedient? So many dreams, so many insatiable desires centered on a nine year old. And the child is already accusing her of suffocating him.

"Peter, Mom wants you to be happy and to do the things you want to do. Not what I want you to do, but what you most desire to do. Mom just wants you to be an honest man."

"Mom, I love you lots."

Peter falls asleep peacefully. Two days later, he is reading a magazine about hunting dogs.

Dreams for Our Children

"I want to give him the world. I want to show him, by my example, how to reach for new horizons. The world is as big or as small as our dreams."

"It's true that I dream that my child will really become someone, that he be successful in life. But what I hope for most is that he will be happy, independent, and will feel that his life is a success."

"That she be happy about who she is, that she be loved, that she appreciate life by doing what she truly likes to do."

"More than anything else, I hope she'll be happy. And no matter what decisions she makes or whatever kind of life she leads, I want to respect her even when I don't agree. My personal dream would be that she learns synchronized swimming."

"I want him to be able to take charge of his life and be able to know the difference between good and evil."

"That he go to school, have a good education, and that he understand the situation his father and I are in, whether we are married or not!"

"That she be kind and not make the mistakes I made."

"I want to give him the fewest 'hangups' possible so that he can be genuine and without problems."

"That her life be beautiful, without drugs or alcohol."

"That he will be a good man, that he will have deep faith; if his faith is strong, he can go through anything. Also, that he will love all those he lives with, and not judge others but help them; that he will see the good things in society. That's hard to do because of all the negative influences that surround us. I dream that my son will give some of his time to teaching others the Word of God. I dream he will become a priest. If that dream isn't realized, I hope he will help others in some way. I will accept him, whatever he becomes."

"He, or she, never stops moving inside of me, and it's wonderful because soon I'll have someone to love for a long time, a long, long time."

"The baby bounces, kicks, moves incessantly, especially when I try to sleep. Boy or girl, I love it already."

"I have two children. It's like having two sorrows and two joys at the same time, two regrets and two satisfactions. Whatever they want to do, I'll try to help them succeed. But I doubt they will pay much attention to my hopes for them."

"It seems to me that, in my situation, the only real chance I can give him is to choose adoption. It seems more important to give

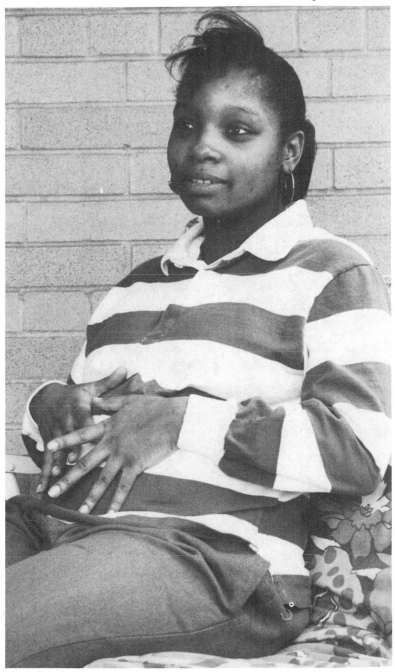

him a chance than to satisfy my personal desire to be a mother."

"I hope he is very successful in his life. I hope he won't always be poor like me. I hope he will settle down, be happy, content with who he is, as I am beginning to be at thirty-five years old. It's not too late!"

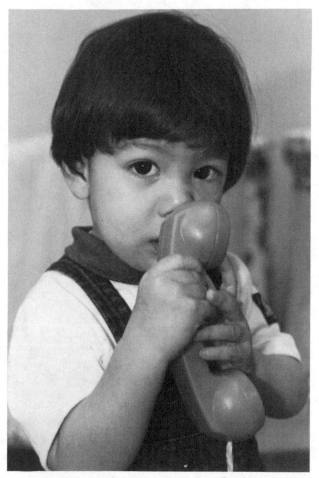

Ben Mark Holzberg

Frank Miller

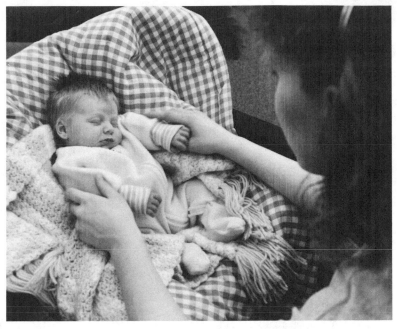

Sleep, My Little One

Sleep, my little one, sleep.
　　Your mother is here and holds your hand.
Sleep, my little one, sleep.

My body is a shield
　　Against the world so cold.
My body is your sun
　　When night comes.
My voice pushes away
　　The terrors that invade your dreams:
　　You're afraid, you're hungry, you're cold.
I am your warmth, your milk, your armor.
In the intimacy of its mother's body, a child finds
　　life.

The Child

Sleep, my little one, sleep.
  All will be well tomorrow.

Life is against you.
You don't have a father;
  He ran when he knew of your presence.
Even your grandparents don't know
  If they will acknowledge you.
Are you the one child too many,
  The unexpected, the unloved, the unplanned?

Sleep, my little one, sleep.
  Life is a dream whose key is sleep.

Welcome to life, my dear little one.
You are already one of the poor
  In the bad section of a bad city.
  The trees are less green,
  The birds less numerous,
  The sun less brilliant.
Will they say that your skin is too dark,
  That your blood is impure,
  Your parentage, doubtful?
Have we had bad luck in the draw?

Sleep, my little one, sleep.
  Don't let fear disturb your sleep;
  Fear is only a lie we tell ourselves.

Sleep, my little one, sleep.
  Life is better than people say.
Your mother isn't alone;
  Other mothers, like her, share the same fate.
Other children, just like you,
  Search in the night for light without end.

The poor possess nothing
   Except life itself
   And the future, and hope.

Sleep, my little one, sleep.
Sleep all through the night.
Tomorrow, we will think about
   The long road of day ahead.
Press yourself close to my heart;
   Warm yourself near my body.
You are my flesh, you are my blood.
Just yesterday, you lived in my body,
   And now here you are facing me.
You are my flesh, you are my blood.
   But you are no longer your mother.
I was only a woman;
   You made me your mother.
You are not only flesh and blood,
   You are already your own person.
My body is your refuge
   For tonight, for other nights,
   But you have a life of your own now.
Sleep, little one, sleep.
Tomorrow it will be your turn
   And together we will find the key to the gardens.

THE PRESENTATION IN THE TEMPLE
(Luke 2:25-35)

And when the day came for them to be purified as laid down by the Law of Moses, they took him up to Jerusalem to present him to the Lord, observing what stands written in the Law of the Lord—every first-born male must be consecrated to the Lord—and also to offer in sacrifice, in accordance with what is said in the Law of the Lord, a pair of turtledoves and two young pigeons. Now in Jerusalem there was a man named Simeon. He was an upright and devout man; he looked forward to Israel's comforting, and the Holy Spirit rested on him. It had been revealed to him by the Holy Spirit that he would not see death until he had set eyes on the Christ of the Lord. Prompted by the Spirit, he came to the Temple; and when the parents brought in the child Jesus to do for him what the Law required, he took him into his arms and blessed God; and he said,

"Now, Master, you can let your servant go in
  peace, just as you promised;
because my eyes have seen the salvation
  which you have prepared for all the nations
  to see,
a light to enlighten the pagans
  and the glory of your people Israel."

As the child's father and mother stood there wondering at the things that were being said about him, Simeon blessed them and said to Mary his mother, "You see this child: he is destined for the fall and for the rising of many in Israel, destined to be a sign that is rejected—and a sword will pierce your own soul too—so that the secret thoughts of many will be laid bare."

6

"Thank You"

Barb Lynch

Barb Lynch

From the Mothers to the Misericordia Sisters

"I simply want to tell you how much I appreciate what you have done for me, and sometimes I think, 'Whatever would I have done if your center didn't exist?' I want you to know that you hold a very important place in my life. I am more grateful than words can say. You're a wonderful group and I love you very much."

"My time here was magnificent, wonderful. I appreciate it very much. It was difficult at first, but it was worth it. I learned so much about life, about love, about myself, and about responsibility. I can't find words to say what I feel. I'm happy, that's all. Thank you."

"I received support, a helping hand when I had to move; I was given food at times when I had nothing. I had a roof over my head when my daughter and I had no place to go. I also had the Sisters' understanding at times when I despaired. There was tenderness when I was sick, and lodging for a month so I could finish my studies."

"I really enjoy being part of the round-table discussions. You have helped us a lot, and you knew how to help our children, too. A big thank you."

"What good fortune to have met you. What I learned and did here was fascinating and fulfilling: school, weaving, ceramics. Thanks to all the Sisters and to

Georgeen Comerford

Paul Hamel, SJ

the staff. Without you, none of it would have been possible. Life looked very grim to me then."

"The Misericordia Sisters gave me immense help when I didn't have anywhere to go. I also believe that the deep communication that exists here among everyone is very important. The classes, celebrations, discussions, and activities are very important because every human being needs to share. We can't go through life alone."

"I like it here. I was warmly welcomed without being asked too many questions and without having to fill out a lot of papers. My private life was respected. In addition, there was always someone available—seven days a week."

"I hope you will continue all you do with so much courage and love and compassion, which I had the chance to experience. I thank you for everything, for all you gave me: life, hope, courage. Thank you, thank you so much. May God help you in all your work."

"The only thing I can say is that I'm very happy to have you near me. I really mean it when I say that. It gives hope to be able to use our talents, to know how to do something in life, to try to understand our children. We're very lucky to have all of you."

RESOURCES
FOR YOUR INNER JOURNEY

WHISPERS OF THE HEART:
A Journey Toward Befriending Yourself
by Dale R. Olen, Ph.D.
Paperbound $8.95, 180 pages, 5½" x 8½"
ISBN 0-89390-100-8
In this book, the author persuasively presents his case that behavior arises from fundamental core energies that are good: the energy to exist, the energy to act freely, the energy to love. Get in touch with these energies and learn to celebrate your own goodness. Your behavior will improve, as well as your sense of fulfillment and growth.

WINNING YOUR INNER BATTLE:
Including Guided Imagery Meditations
by Jeanne Heiberg
Paperbound $8.95, 152 pages, 5½" x 8½"
ISBN 0-89390-159-8
Life is full of external dangers and problems. However, the greater battleground is with our own thoughts, feelings, and attitudes. The author, using her personal experiences, shows you how to win the inner battle by taming your internal dragons and turning them into allies for life's journey. Each chapter ends with a guided imagery meditation that you can use yourself or in a group.

FEEDING THE SPIRIT: How to Create Your Own Ceremonial Rites, Festivals, and Celebrations
by Nancy Brady Cunningham
Paperbound $7.95, 118 pages, 5½" x 8½"
ISBN 0-89390-117-2
Combine ancient rites and modern-day practicality with these 24 ceremonies you can celebrate in your own home. Ceremonies such as Dream Making, Color Meditation, and Moon Magic will inspire you to create your own rituals; the solstice and equinox celebrations will add a special air to each season.

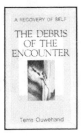

THE DEBRIS OF THE ENCOUNTER: A Recovery of Self
by Terre Ouwehand
Paperbound $7.95, 78 pages, 5½" x 8½"
ISBN 0-89390-137-7
During a period of psychotherapeutic exploration, Terre Ouwehand began meditating and experienced what psychologists call eidetic imagery or what mystics call inner visions. *The Debris of the Encounter* is her story of recovery and healing. Ouwehand, a gifted playwright, works with bold images to convey an unfolding sense of a higher power at work in her life.

Order from your bookseller or use the order form on the last page.

NEW

FOR
WORKING
WITH TEENS

ACTING IT OUT
74 Short Plays for Starting Discussions with Teenagers
by Joan Sturkie and Marsh Cassady
Paperbound $21.95, 357 pages, 6" x 9"
ISBN 0-89390-178-4

Getting teenagers to talk about how they're feeling can be frustrating. Acting It Out offers a new approach: 74 short plays for starting discussions for teenagers. Teens act out a short play then, through questions provided at the end of each drama, they discuss how the characters in the play dealt with the particular issue. The attention is focused on the characters and the issue rather than the teens themselves. These dramas address challenging subjects: abortion, suicide, child abuse, gangs, home life, drugs, etc. They don't gloss over the realities teens face today; rather they present the issues in a straightforward manner and will encourage your teens to talk about them in the same way.

Excerpt from a play about sexual abuse:

Barbara: I should have suspected, but I didn't. Looking back, I see that he started paying a lot more attention to me six months or so before this happened. He was always a loving man with Mom and Peter and me. But when he kissed me, it was just a little too long. When he hugged me, I'd start to feel uncomfortable and try to pull away. But he acted hurt, so I didn't make a big deal out of it.

Dixie: Look, Barbara, someone's going to have to report this. You realize that, don't you?

Barbara: I know. But then what? What's going to happen to my family?

Order from your bookseller, or use the order form on the last page.

COUNSELING
AND PEER COUNSELING

R E S O U R C E S

CALL TO COMFORT:
A Counseling Manual for Every Christian
by Tom Yarbrough
Paperbound $7.95, 131 pages, 5½" x 8½"
ISBN 0-89390-119-9
By combining biblical principles, personal anecdotes, and psychological tools, the author shows you how to prepare for informal counseling and what 'equipment' you need. In addition, he shows you specific steps for your first counseling endeavor and provides a work manual containing extra help.

LISTENING WITH LOVE:
True Stories from Peer Counseling
(Revised Edition)
by Joan Sturkie
Clothbound $16.95, ISBN 0-89390-151-2
Paperbound $9.95, 255 pages 6" x 9"
ISBN 0-89390-150-4
This book tells about peer helping: a program that trains young people to help each other. Includes section on how to start and maintain such a program. These stories from the lives of actual students can be used in class (with Teacher's Guide) to generate discussion of problems which are universal among young people today.

TEACHER'S GUIDE TO LISTENING WITH LOVE
Paperbound $9.95, 64 pages, 5½" x 8½"
ISBN 0-89390-161-X

THE PEER COUNSELOR'S POCKET BOOK
by Joan Sturkie and Valerie Gibson
Paperbound $9.95, 74 pages, 4¼" x 7"
ISBN 0-89390-162-8
The peer counselor's basic tool, a handy guide and reference book for pocket or purse that includes the essentials of peer counseling in a quick, easy to find form.

Order from your bookseller, or use the order form on the last page.

STORIES
for Growth and Change

BIBLICAL BLUES: Growing Through Set-Ups and Let-Downs
by Andre Papineau
Paperbound $7.95, 229 pages, 5½" x 8½"
ISBN 0-89390-157-1
The twenty-five stories in this book address incidents you may have experienced: betrayal, divorce, death of a loved one, greed, paranoia, loneliness. This book will help you recover from your setups and letdowns by evaluating each situation, analyzing your feelings, and helping you to eventually move on.

JESUS ON THE MEND: Healing Stories for Ordinary People
by Andre Papineau
Paperbound $7.95, 150 pages, 5½" x 8½"
ISBN 0-89390-140-7
Here are 18 Gospel-based stories that illustrate four aspects of healing: Acknowledging the Need, Reaching Out for Help, The Healer's Credentials, and The Healer's Therapy. Also included are helpful reflections following each story, focusing on the process of healing that takes place. If you better understand healing, like Jesus you can bring comfort to those who hurt.

BREAKTHROUGH: Stories of Conversion
by Andre Papineau
Paperbound $7.95, 139 pages, 5½" x 8½"
ISBN 0-89390-128-8
Here is an essential resource for RCIA, Cursillo, and renewal programs. You and your group will witness what takes place inside Papineau's characters as they change. These stories will remind you that change, ultimately, is a positive experience. You'll find reflections from a psychological point of view following each section to help you help others deal with their personal conversions.

ORDER FORM --

Order from your local bookstore, or mail this form to:

Qty	Title	Price	Total
___	_____	_____	_____
___	_____	_____	_____
___	_____	_____	_____
___	_____	_____	_____
___	_____	_____	_____

Subtotal _____
CA residents add 6¼% sales tax _____
*Postage and handling _____
Total amount enclosed _____

*Postage and handling
$1.50 for orders under $10.00
$2.00 for orders of $10.00-$25.00
9% (max. $7.00) of order for orders over $25.00

Resource Publications, Inc.
160 E. Virginia St., Suite 290
San Jose, Ca 95112
408 286-8505
FAX 408 287-8748

☐ My check or purchase order is enclosed.
☐ Charge my ☐ Visa ☐ MC Exp. date _____

Card #____-_____-_____-_____

Signature _____

Name: _____
Institution: _____
Street: _____
City: _____ St___ Zip_____
Code: AR